NOVELLO HANDEL
General Editor Watkins Shaw

THREE VESPER PSALMS, NO.1
Dixit Dominus

Psalm 110 for two sopranos, alto, tenor & bass soli,
SSATB, strings & continuo
Edited by Watkins Shaw

vocal score (latin text)

Order No: NOV 072323

NOVELLO PUBLISHING LIMITED

PREFACE

This work, a product of Handel's sojourn in Italy as a young man, was completed in 1707, and is one of several pieces of Latin church music of that period by him. Vincent Novello, who possessed a manuscript score of three of them (*Dixit Dominus*, *Laudate pueri*, and *Nisi Dominus*), was the first to point out that these are psalms appointed for Vespers. Going further, James S. Hall ('The Problem of Handel's Latin Church Music', *The Musical Times*, Vol. 100 (1959), pp. 197-200) has argued that all Handel's Latin church music taken together constitutes a setting of Vespers for the Feast of Our Lady of Mount Carmel in 1707.

Faint echoes of *Dixit Dominus* were in Handel's mind when he came to compose the 'Utrecht' *Te Deum*, as witness the opening phrase of 'Dominus a dextris tuis' (cf. 'The glorious company of the apostles') and the instrumental and choral texture of 'De torrente in via bibet' (cf. 'We believe that thou shalt come'), though too much should not be made of the former similarity, the melodic curve and harmonic implications of which are a commonplace of baroque musical facture.

Sources

A London, British Library (Reference Division), RM 20.f.1, ff. 30-82v, in the composer's hand, dated Rome, April 1707.

B Manchester Public Library, Henry Watson Library, MS 130 Hd4.v.205, pp. 1-191. Score, originally belonging to Charles Jennens, in whose family it remained until acquired by Sir Newman Flower in 1918.

C London, Royal College of Music, Parry Room Library, MS 246. An 18th-century score, formerly No. 1616 of the Sacred Harmonic Society Library.

D London, Royal College of Music, Parry Room Library, MS 248. Score, formerly belonging successively to Dragonetti, Vincent Novello, and the Sacred Harmonic Society (No. 1618).

E London, Royal College of Music, Parry Room Library, MS 249. Score, formerly belonging to the Concert of Antient Music.

B, C, D, and E add nothing significant to an understanding of the text, and this edition is based on A. In addition to *Dixit Dominus*, B, D, and E also contain *Laudate pueri* and *Nisi Dominus*.

Editorial procedure

Small-size notes and square brackets indicate editorial matter. Horizontal square brackets and quaver beams across bar-lines are editorial indications of a rhythmic regrouping in triple time. The division into movements is editorial. Handel's C clefs for soprano, alto, and tenor voices have here been transcribed in the G clef, and his time-signature **C** has been rendered as $\frac{4}{4}$.

On the basis of a fair amount of experience by now in editing Handel's music, I have concluded that it is unnecessary to distinguish as editorial by far the greater number of accidentals and ties omitted by him. In the music of (for example) Purcell or Weelkes, not only an editorial conscience but also a considerable degree of dubiety make such distinction of accidentals a matter of significance. But with Handel all that is needed is such tidying up of his score as a modern publishing house would do as a matter of course when seeing a new composition through the press. Time and time again, to take a typical instance, Handel, writing with two flats in the signature, will reach D minor and write the dominant chord with a sharp to C but forgetting the natural to E, as he would also do in such a group as

Is it really necessary to show that Handel forgot the naturals required by this passage?

(No. 1, bar 37)

Throughout the present work there are but three instances where there is to my mind a shadow of doubt, and these are duly marked by square brackets (p. 28, bar 70, p. 38, bar 6, and p. 54, bar 17); and I have placed yet one more accidental in square brackets (p. 81, bar 79), not because I feel any doubt but in case anyone should compare my text with that of Chrysander. For the rest the context, or the doubling of another voice or instrument, settles the matter clearly. So also with ties in Handel's music. Is anything gained by festooning these pages with special marks, of which a very large number would be required, for this sort of thing?

(No. 1, bars 34-35, Vln. I)

Do -

(No. 2, bars 15-16)

In one passage alone—even here, perhaps, unnecessarily—I have shown the ties I have supplied, that is to say in the course of bars 1-15 and 137-148 of No. 6.

If, in taking this decision not to distinguish accidentals and ties omitted by Handel, I incur any disapprobation, I am prepared to accept that. And if there be any risk in reserving to myself the decision whether or not any particular case is one of doubt, then I face it rather than decorate a vocal score with very many instances indeed of typographical distinction where no possible doubt can arise.

Handel's dots in the voice parts

On pp. 63-64 I have exactly reproduced the dots which Handel unsystematically applied to the crotchets sung to a continuous vowel in that movement. Be it remembered, however, that for a true *staccato* Handel would have used a vertical dash, the dot not forming part of his notation for that purpose. His present dots, therefore, indicate simply renewed articulation, not a shortened note-value; and they apply to all crotchets for the third syllable of 'con-quas-sa-bit', whether so marked or not.

The keyboard part

The keyboard part in this vocal score is designed solely for rehearsal accompaniment, and not for purposes of performance on the organ in the absence of an orchestra. It supplies in outline the necessary harmonic support with an indication of the rhythmic figuration, but it is nowhere near a short score from which the idiomatic 5-part string texture can be extracted.

Small-size notes indicate an editorial working of the basso continuo; but for vocal score purposes it has not been thought necessary to supply chords above such bass notes as, for example, the second and third beats of bar 38 in No. 1, though these would be needed in a performance with orchestra.

In laying out this keyboard part, however, particular care has been taken to show clearly, and in its exact form, the basso continuo. Where, in Handel's MS(A), this passes into the C clef (for a *bassetti* passage), the G clef has been used here. However, the bass of bars 34-36 in No. 9 is a true orchestral bass and was *not* written in the C clef; but to have maintained the F clef would have created great difficulty in expressing the rehearsal accompaniment on two staves.

The rehearsal accompaniment to Nos. 5 and 6 presents special features. In No. 5 the strings are occupied for the most part in doubling the voices. If similar support is required at rehearsal, the accompanist should play from the open vocal score. Instead of printing this in short score (in which form the 5-part texture is far more trouble than in open score), I have provided a simple continuo-type harmony. In No. 6 from bar 81 the four upper strings duplicate the basso continuo. This feature is shown here on a separate stave, to enable the rehearsal accompanist to use it as desired, while the keyboard staves are used to convey the continuo harmony.

Acknowledgements

I gratefully acknowledge the permission of the British Library to base this edition on **A** above, and offer my thanks also to Manchester Public Library for being allowed to have a microfilm of **B**.

WATKINS SHAW
1977

PSALM 110

I

No. 1 Dixit Dominus Domino meo: Sede a dextris meis, donec ponam inimicos tuos, scabellum pedum tuorum.

II

No. 2 Virgam virtutis tuae, emittet Dominus ex Sion: dominare in medio inimicorum tuorum.

III

No. 3 Tecum principium in die virtutis tuae in splendoribus sanctorum: ex utero ante luciferum genui te.

IV

No. 4 Juravit Dominus, et non poenitebit eum:
No. 5 Tu es sacerdos in aeternum secundum ordinem Melchisedech.

V

No. 6 Dominus a dextris tuis, confregit in die irae suae reges.

VI

No. 7 Judicabit in nationibus, implebit ruinas: conquassabit capita in terra multorum.

VII

No. 8 De torrente in via bibet: propterea exaltabit caput.

No. 9 Gloria Patri, et Filio, et Spiritui Sancto: sicut erat in principio et nunc, et semper, et in saecula saeculorum.   Amen.

This Psalm is by no means easy to understand in the English of either the Book of Common Prayer or the Authorized Version of the Bible. It is helpful to consult the Revised Standard Version of the Bible and the New English Bible.

DURATION ABOUT 40 MINUTES

Full score and instrumental material,
including a complete keyboard continuo part,
are available on hire.

DIXIT DOMINUS

Edited by Watkins Shaw

G. F. HANDEL

1 Dixit Dominus
Chorus

1) Throughout the work, except for some violoncello passages in the bass, Handel failed to specify the instruments, but 5-part strings are understood. In his autograph score each 'viola' part has a separate stave, the lower with Tenor C clef.

2) Bar 7, Vln. I. Handel inadvertently prefixed a flat to this a^2.

20234

3) Bar 12, Basso continuo. Handel at first wrote both crotchets as *d*, figured ♯, later changing them to what is given here. He forgot, however, to make the corresponding change to bar 132.

20234

3

20234

4

4) Handel wrote 'Violoncello' but it has been contracted throughout to Cello.

de a dex-tris me - is,

Solo

Se-de,

Solo

31

se - - - -

34

5) Bars 67-9, Tenor. Handel's verbal underlay is not clear.

6) Bar 91. Handel wrote his 'tutti' direction against the second semiquaver of the bar, where Vln.I alone is playing.

16

18

7) Bar 127. See bar 7.

8) Bar 133, Basso continuo. Both crotchets *d*, figured ♯ in A, but see note to bar 12.

2 Virgam virtutis
Solo

ALTO

Vir-gam vir-tu - tis, —— vir-tu-tis tu - ae,

vir-gam vir-tu - tis, —— vir-tu-tis tu - ae, e - mit - tet

Do-mi-nus, e - mit-tet Do-mi-nus ex Si - on, e-mit-tet Do -

mi-nus ex Si -

on: do-mi - na - - - - -

- - - - - - -

A

- re in me - - - - di-o i -

in me-di-o i - ni - mi - co - - rum tu-o-rum. i - ni - mi-co-

- - - - - rum tu-o -

[tr]

rum, i - ni - mi - co - - - - rum tu-

o - rum.

[tr]

[mf]

[rit.]

3 Tecum principium

Solo

SOPRANO

Te - cum prin - ci - pi - um in — di - e — vir - tu - tis,

Cello   Tutti Solo   Tutti

in — di - e — vir - tu - tis, — vir - tu - tis — tu - ae

Solo   Tutti

1) Bar 1 (and throughout): ♩ ♩ ♪ ♩ ♩ = ♩ ♪³ ♪ ♩

2) Bar 8 (and throughout): ♩. ♪ ♪ ♩ = 9/8 ♩. ♩ ♪ ♩.

3) Bars 27-28: $\frac{9}{8}$ ♩. ♩ ♪♩. ♩ ♪♩. ♩ ♪

4) Bar 31: $\frac{9}{8}$ ♩. ♩ ♪♩ ♪

rum, in splen-do-ri-bus san-cto-rum.

34 Solo Tutti

Te - cum_ prin - ci-pi-um in di - e vir-tu - tis,__ vir-tu - tis

39 Solo Tutti Solo Tutti

tu - ae in_ splen-do - -

44

- - - -

48

5) Bar 35:
6) Bar 41:

28

ri - bus san - cto - rum.

52 Solo

Tutti

Te - cum prin -

57

3

6
4+

6
4+
2

4

Solo

8)

ci - pi - um in di - e - vir - tu - tis, vir - tu - tis tu - ae in splen -

62

p

[Tutti]

do - - - - -

68

7) Bars 54-55, 59-60: 9/8 ♩. ♩ ♪♪ ♪ | ♪♪♪ ♩.

8) Bars 62-63: 9/8 ♩. ♩ ♪♪. | ♩. ♩. ♩ ♪

20234

9) Bar 73: $\frac{9}{8}$ 𝅗𝅥. ♩ ♪♪ ♪

10) Bars 79 - end: rhythmic alteration (quasi $\frac{9}{8}$) throughout.

4 Juravit Dominus
Chorus

1) consecutive octaves *sic*

5 Tu es sacerdos

Chorus

1) See p. v for a note about the rehearsal accompaniment to this movement.

40

20234

A
-di-nem Mel-chi - - se-dech, se-cun-dum or-di-nem Mel-
chi - se-dech, Mel-chi - se-dech,
se-cun-dum or-di-nem Mel-chi-se-dech, se-cun-dum
in ae - ter - num se-cun-dum or-di-nem Mel-chi-se-dech,
tu es sa - cer - dos
A
18
chi-se-dech, se-cun-dum or-di-nem Mel-chi -
se-cun-dum or-di-nem Mel-chi-se-dech, Mel-chi - - se - dech,
or-di-nem Mel-chi-se-dech, se-cum-dum or-di-nem Mel-chi - se-dech, se-cun-dum
se - cun - dum or - - - di -
in ae - ter - - - - -
20

42

6 Dominus a dextris tuis
Soli and Chorus

1) See p. v for a note about the rehearsal accompaniment to this movement.

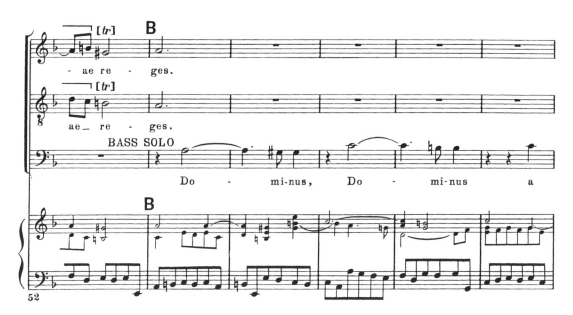

dex - tris tu - is, con - fre - - - -

- - git in di - e i - rae su - ae_ re -

ges, con-fre - - - -

C

- git in di - e i - rae su - ae_ re -

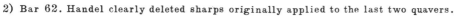

2) Bar 62. Handel clearly deleted sharps originally applied to the last two quavers.

4) Where the violins are in octaves with the bass, the violas double now the bass, now the violins. Where the violins are two octaves above the bass, the violas take the intermediate octave.

50

105

111

4) Bar 106, Basso continuo. 2nd note G in the source.

20234

in di - e i-rae su - ae re - ges.

in di - e i-rae su - ae re - ges.

in di - e i-rae su - ae re - ges.

in di - e i-rae su - ae re - ges.

in di - e i-rae su - ae re - ges.

Vln. I

129

Vln. I

Vln. II

Cont.

135

7

6
5

6
5

[tr]

141

7   4+ 7   4

7 Judicabit in nationibus
Chorus

1) Bar 7. Inadvertently Handel figured this minim 4 3.

54

58

34

37

60

*Handel's careless figuring.

20234

62

20234

64

con-quas-sa-bit, con-quas-sa-bit, con-quas-sa-bit, con-quas-sa - bit, con-quas-

con-quas-sa-bit, con-quas-sa-bit, con-quas-sa-bit, con-quas-sa - bit, con-quas-

con-quas-sa-bit, con-quas-sa-bit, con-quas-sa-bit, con-quas-sa - bit, con-quas-

con-quas-sa-bit, con-quas-sa-bit, con-quas-sa-bit, con-quas-sa - bit, con-quas-

con-quas-sa-bit, con-quas-sa-bit, con-quas-sa-bit, con-quas-sa - bit, con-quas-

74

sa - - - bit,

sa - - - bit,

sa - - - bit,

sa - - - bit,

sa - - - bit,

80

6
4
2+

7
#

20234

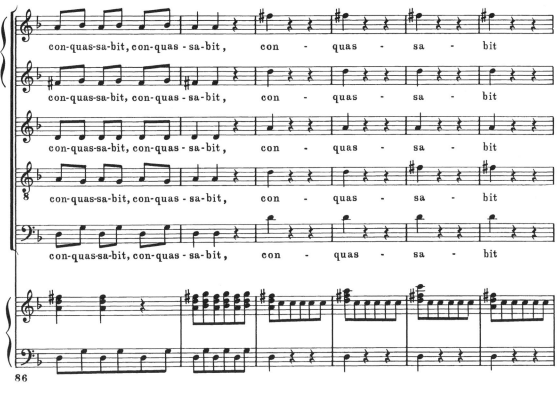

con-quas-sa-bit, con-quas - sa-bit, con - quas - sa - bit
con-quas-sa-bit, con-quas - sa-bit, con - quas - sa - bit
con-quas-sa-bit, con-quas - sa - bit, con - quas - sa - bit
con-quas-sa-bit, con-quas - sa - bit, con - quas - sa - bit
con-quas-sa-bit, con-quas - sa-bit, con - quas - sa - bit

86

ca - pi-ta in ter - ra_ mul-to - rum, con-quas-sa -
ca - pi-ta in ter - ra mul-to - rum, con-quas-sa -
ca - pi-ta in ter - ra mul-to - rum, con-quas-sa -
ca - pi-ta in ter - ra_ mul-to - rum, con-quas-sa -
ca - pi-ta in ter - ra_ mul-to - rum, con-quas-sa -

92

- - bit, con - quas - sa - bit
- - bit, con - quas - sa - bit
- - bit, con - quas - sa - bit
- - bit, con - quas - sa - bit
- - bit, con - quas - sa - bit

98

ca - pi-ta in ter - ra _ mul-to - rum.
ca - pi-ta in ter - ra mul-to - rum.
ca - pi-ta in ter - ra mul-to - rum.
ca - pi-ta in ter - ra _ mul-to - rum.
ca - pi-ta in ter - ra _ mul-to - rum.

105

8 De torrente in via bibet
Soli and Chorus

1) Here and elsewhere in this movement apparent consecutive 5ths and 8ves arise in short score where the string parts cross.

2) The rehearsal pianist may well take these and corresponding bass crotchets an octave lower.

9 Gloria Patri

Chorus

et Spi-ri-tu-i San-cto, et Spi-ri-tu-i San - cto.

Glo - - -

- - ri-u, glo-ri-u Pa - - -

- - - - - tri, Pa - tri,et Fi-li-o,

29

31

1) Bars 34-36 exceptionally use the G clef in this edition for the continuo; see p. v.

42

45

78

C

per, si-cut e-rat in prin-ci-pi-o, et nunc, ___ et sem - per.

per, si-cut e-rat in prin-ci-pi-o, et nunc, et nunc, et sem - per.

- ri-a si-cut e-rat in prin-ci-pi-o, et nunc, et nunc, et sem - per.

cto, si-cut e-rat in prin-ci-pi-o, et nunc, et sem - per.

cto, si-cut e-rat in prin-ci-pi-o, et nunc, et nunc, et sem - per.

C

52

Allegro [♩ = 88]
S I

Et in sae-cu-la sae-cu-lo-rum a-men, a - - - -

S II

Et in sae-cu-la sae-cu-lo-rum a-men, a - - - -

Allegro [♩ = 88]

55

(SI)

(SII)

A

Et in sae-cu-la sae-cu-lo-rum a-men, a - - -

59

80

20234

82

81

84

2) Bar 81, Tenor (and Vla.). A has ♮ to *e'*.

20234

86

105

108

20234

sae-cu-lo-rum a-men, a - - -

sae-cu-lo-rum a-men, a - -

a - -

sae - cu-la sae-cu-lo-rum amen, a -

sae - cu-la sae-cu-lo-rum amen, a - -

112

115

3) Bar 135, Tenor. Handel wrote crotchet d^1 only.

92

154

158

S. D. G.
G. F. Hendel
1707
li d'Aprile
Roma

Printed and bound in Great Britain by
Caligraving Limited Thetford Norfolk

CHORAL WORKS FOR MIXED VOICES

BACH
CHRISTMAS ORATORIO
For soprano, alto, tenor & bass soli, SATB & orchestra
MASS IN B MINOR
For two sopranos, alto, tenor & bass soli, SSATB & orchestra
ST MATTHEW PASSION
For soprano, alto, tenor & bass soli, SATB & orchestra

BRAHMS
REQUIEM
For soprano & baritone soli, SATB & orchestra

ELGAR
GIVE UNTO THE LORD PSALM 29
For SATB & organ or orchestra

FAURE
ed Desmond Ratcliffe
REQUIEM
For soprano & baritone soli, SATB & orchestra

HANDEL
ed Watkins Shaw
MESSIAH
For soprano, alto, tenor & bass soli, SATB & orchestra

HAYDN
CREATION
For soprano, tenor & bass soli, SATB & orchestra
IMPERIAL 'NELSON' MASS
For soprano, alto, tenor & bass soli, SATB & orchestra
MARIA THERESA MASS
For soprano, alto, tenor & bass soli, SATB & orchestra
MASS IN TIME OF WAR 'PAUKENMESSE'
For soprano, alto, tenor & bass soli,i SATB & orchestra

MONTEVERDI
ed Denis Stevens & John Steele
BEATUS VIR
For soloists, double choir, organ & orchestra
ed John Steele
MAGNIFICAT
For SSATB chorus, instruments & organ
ed Denis Stevens
VESPERS
For soloists, double choir, organ & orchestra

MOZART
REQUIEM MASS
For soprano, alto, tenor & bass soli, SATB & orchestra

SCARLATTI
ed John Steele
DIXIT DOMINUS
For SATB, soli & chorus, string orchestra & organ continuo